GW01319417

Dots & Grids

Helen Pengelly

ASHTON SCHOLASTIC
SYDNEY AUCKLAND NEW YORK TORONTO LONDON

The purchase of this book entitles the teacher to reproduce
the blackline masters for classroom use.

Typeset by David Lake Typesetting, Forresters Beach NSW.
Printed by Globalcom Pty Ltd, Singapore.
Typeset in Helvetica.
12 11 10 9 8 7 6 5 4 3 2 1   1 2 3 4 5 / 9

Setting the context

This book is one in a series of books addressing mathematics curricula in the primary school years. Collectively, the books outline an approach to the teaching and learning of mathematics. Their purpose is to inform, support and resource teachers when planning, implementing and reviewing their mathematics programs.

Giving information about the rationale, content and methodology in a conceptual rather than a procedural way enables teachers to build a curriculum which is responsive to the needs of individual children, the class, the school and the school community. The materials do not provide a program in the traditional sense of setting learning out in a linear and prescribed manner through student books and teacher guides. They do provide teachers with a framework to build a mathematics curriculum which reflects the rationale and methodology of the different education department policy guidelines. Learning mathematics becomes a personal, interactive process negotiated between the policy statements of the institution and the school, the interests, abilities and reactions of the children in a class, and the teacher's belief, knowledge and practices.

One book discusses the principles underlying this approach to mathematics teaching. Six topic books give an account of these theories in action. They describe the nature and type of activities which give children personal experiences with mathematics. The books outline an ongoing process of planning for and responding to children's mathematical learning.

In another collection of books in this series, a group of teachers write about how they implemented this approach. Their books on getting started, on planning and programming, on assessment, evaluation and reporting, and on the role of language and interaction in mathematics learning, are practical accounts of organisation and management strategies. Books in the fourth category are to be used to resource students' mathematical learning in an active way.

How to use

Dots & Grids

Pages of dot and grid paper are useful in mathematics classes. This book consists of a selection of both in various sizes. These masters can be photocopied and used whenever considered appropriate. Teachers may wish to have a range available so that children can choose which ones are most appropriate to their current mathematical investigations or decide which ones provide a suitable framework to represent their thoughts.

The grids have many different purposes. They may aid geometrical constructions, be used to explore similarity and congruence, and provide a framework for drawing nets for solids. They are also useful when working with factors, multiples, primes, composites, area, perimeter and surface area.

Children use dot paper to record the shapes they have constructed on geoboards. Dot paper is also another way of creating outlines for geometric constructions. Children may also find dot paper useful to record work they do with fractions, tessellations and symmetrical designs.

Geometric constructions

If children are constructing three-dimensional shapes from grid or dot outlines, the masters should be copied onto cardboard to give the cutout shapes added strength. Isometric dot paper and the triangular and hexagonal grids encourage more complex constructions. Challenging children to make shapes that are twice (three, four, or . . . times) the size of an original shape opens the way for investigating surface area, volume, exponential growth, similarity and congruence. When investigating these ideas, children search for patterns in the data they collect and develop rules to form generalisations from their experiences.

Nets for solids

Children can either use dot or grid sheets to make nets before constructing three-dimensional shapes, or use them to draw nets for existing three-dimensional models. Once again, if a shape is to be constructed, it is best to copy the grid or dot design onto cardboard.

Factors, multiples, primes and composites

To learn about factors, multiples, primes and composites, children make rectangular arrays (filled-in rectangles) using square tiles. In the process of doing this they learn the multiplication tables. Four tiles, for example, can be arranged as 1x4, 2x2 or 4x1, while 12 forms six different arrays—1x12, 2x6, 3x4, 4x3, 6x2 and 12x1. When children first start to record these arrays they draw diagrams of them. This freehand drawing takes time. Grid paper can be used to provide an outline for recording arrays. This paper makes the process of recording much quicker and more precise. Lighter grid paper makes it easier for children to see the images they draw.

After a great deal of experience forming rectangles with tiles and recording the arrays, children eventually find that the same arrays can be created by simply drawing them on grid paper. Manipulating tiles is no longer necessary. The squares on the grid take their place. Children decide when they no longer need to physically manipulate the tiles. Mentally operating with this data makes the process of finding all the arrays for numbers beyond 20 more efficient. Eventually they begin to numerically represent the arrays as the multiplication of two adjacent sides, eg 3 by 4 or 3x4.

Children spend a great deal of time making arrays and collecting data. In the process, they learn the multiplication tables. You hear children muttering to themselves things like, 'No, it won't be two because two doesn't go into 15', or, 'It can't have a side edge of two because 21 is an odd number'.

Once children have collected information about the numbers up to 50 or 100, and checked their results with others in the class or on a calculator, they classify the information. Some numbers have only two arrays. These are all the prime numbers. Some have an odd number of arrays. These are square numbers. Shapes which form an array with a base edge of two make up the even numbers and those that do not are all odd. Grid paper helps children gather and organise the data which they later reflect upon to come to these conclusions. This is described in more detail in *The nature of* **Number**.

Area and perimeter

Children link their experiences of making arrays with finding the area and perimeter of rectangular shapes. Through collecting and recording data about the dimensions of rectangular shapes, children realise that the area is the base edge multiplied by the side edge, and the perimeter is twice the sum of these two sides. Children may also use grid paper to find that the area of a triangle is half the area of its enclosing rectangle. How children investigate this is described more fully in **Measuring Space**.

Children copy or draw shapes on grid paper and count how many squares are in each shape. The grid paper can be copied onto transparencies and used as an overlay. Instead of copying shapes onto paper, place the grid transparency over the shape and count the squares. This makes measuring the surface of many three-dimensional shapes much easier.

Measuring shapes with different sized grids helps children to learn that the unit of the measure affects the result of the measure. The larger the unit, the smaller the numerical description of the area.

Representing shapes on geoboards

Dot paper is used by children to represent the shapes they make on geoboards. They can be given tasks such as, 'How many different three- (four-, five-, . . .) sided shapes can you make on the geoboard. Record.' Grid paper is just one of the ways children may choose to represent their shapes. They could also reconstruct the shapes by matching the length of each side with straws.

When children first use geoboards they tend to select recording paper which has dots spaced the same as the ones on the board. Once confident with the spatial relationships, they can use dot paper with smaller dimensions. Children should be the ones to make this choice.

Exploring patterns

The grids of specified dimensions (4x4, 5x5, . . .) can be used for exploring patterns. For example, a child might select a particular grid, repeatedly write their first name across that grid, and find out what pattern exists by colouring in the last letter of their name. The child can then find out what happens (and why) to the pattern when other sized grids are used.

The ten by ten grid can be used to write numbers in groups of 100, up to 1000.

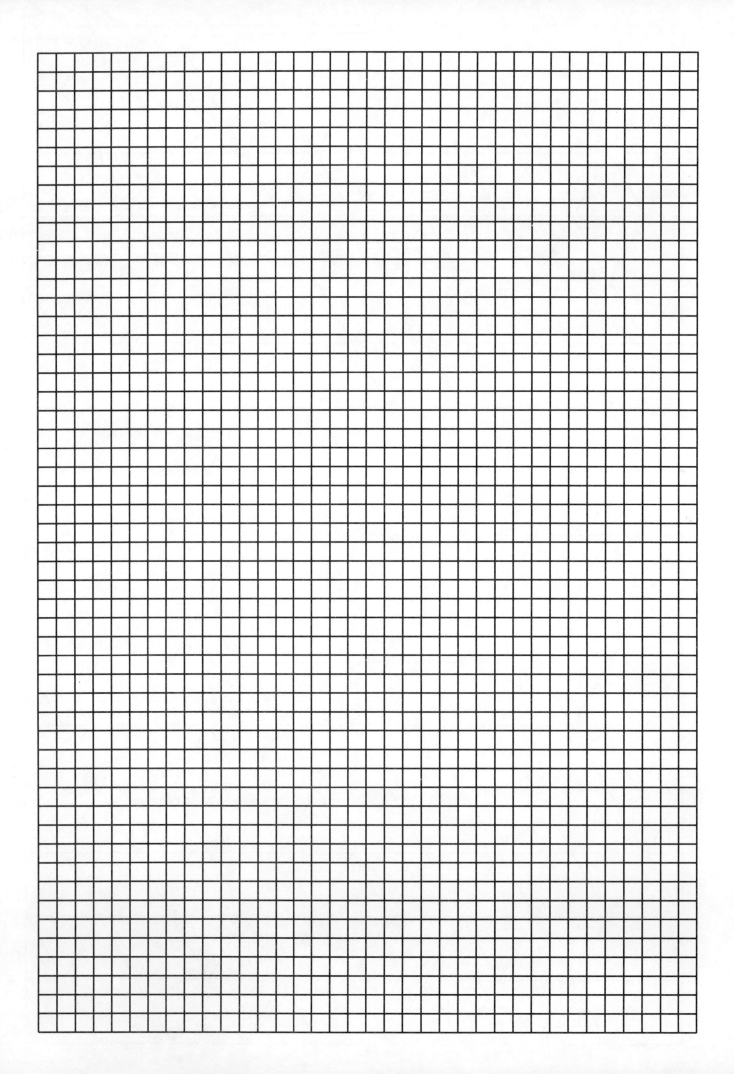

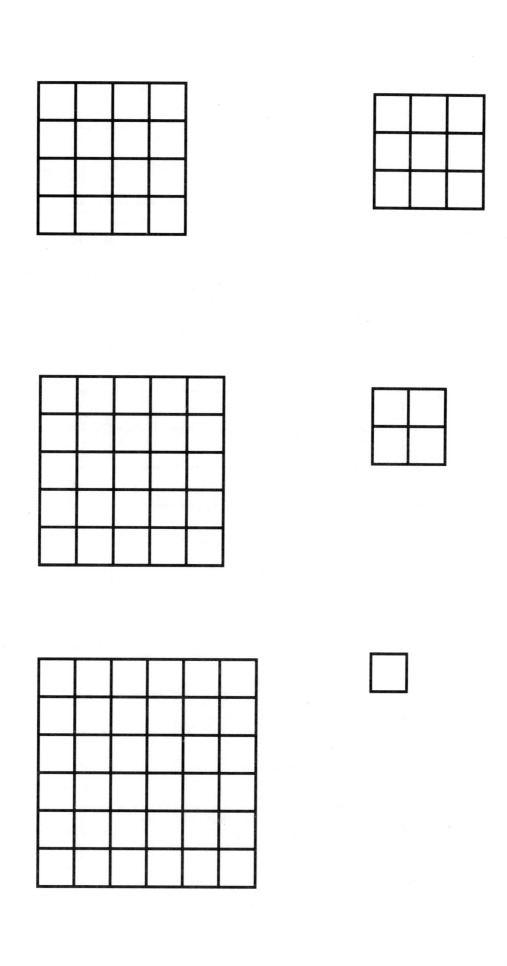

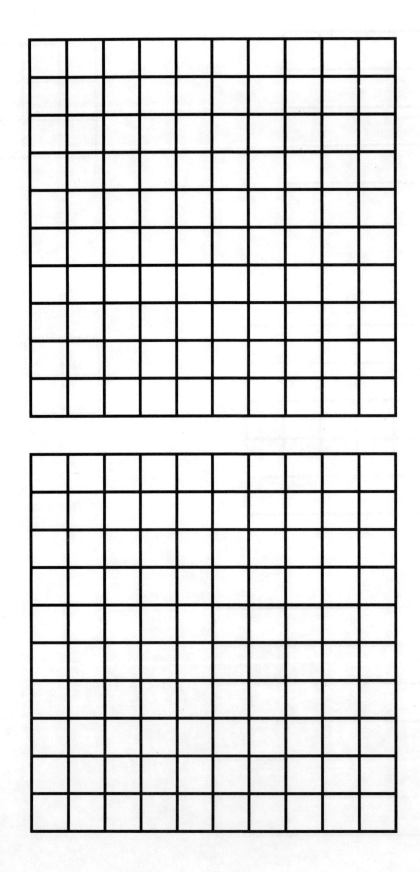

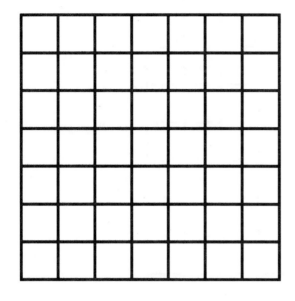

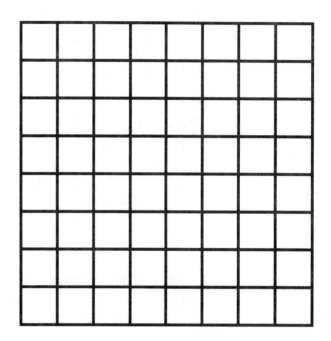

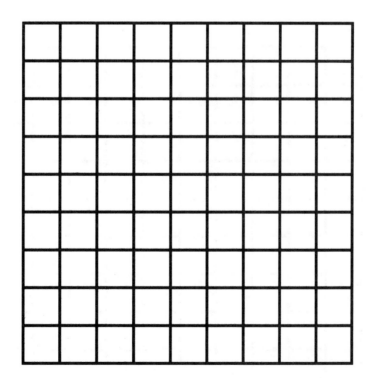

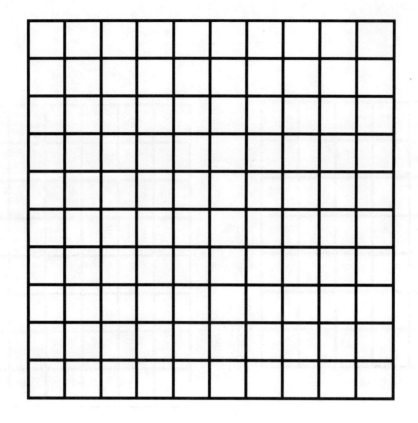

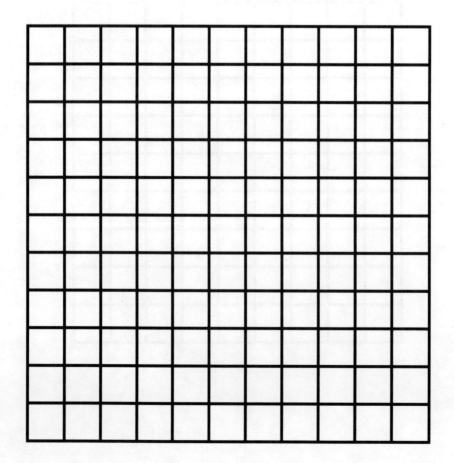

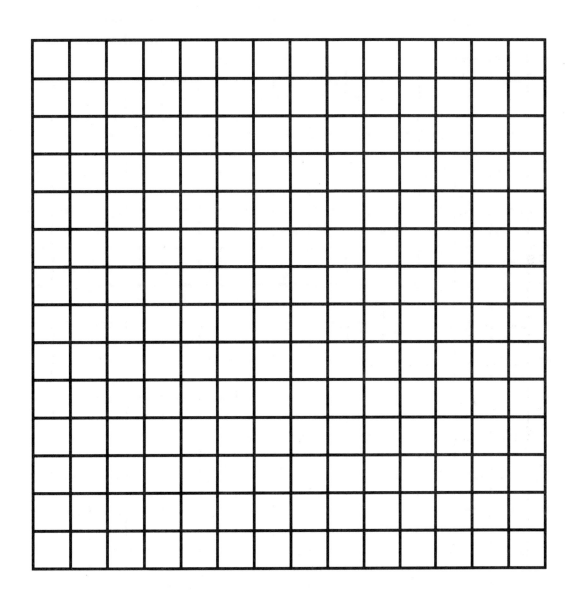

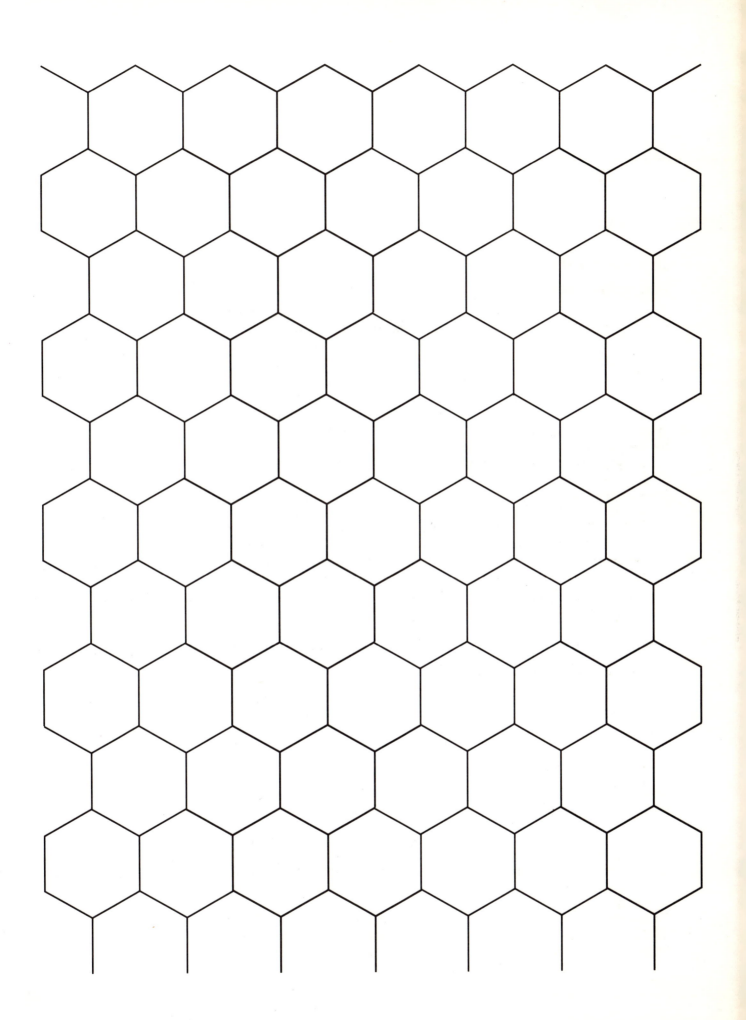

Books in this series

Rationale statement

The principles which govern this approach to mathematics teaching and learning are described in **Mapping mathematical meaning**. This theoretical statement provides the rationale for the way of teaching mathematics that is outlined in the other materials in this series.

Teaching and learning

Six topic books, **Base Ten**, *understanding the structure of the number system; Mathematics, a search for* **Patterns**; **Classification**, *a process for learning mathematics; Making sense of* **Fractions**; *The nature of* **Number**; and **Measuring Space**, give an account of these theories in action. These books are practical descriptions of activities and resources a teacher can use to establish a mathematical environment. They also discuss the types of response children make to such experiences, as well as map the development in children's mathematical thinking. Ongoing information about how to adapt and modify an activity to respond to children's developing thoughts provides the framework for continuity in learning. It also acts to challenge and support children's thinking beyond their existing parameters.

Managing the curriculum

A group of teachers implementing this approach have reflected on their classroom experiences. Their books provide practical information about how to manage aspects of the curriculum.

In these books, teachers share the structures and strategies they have developed to make the organisation and management of this approach to teaching effective and efficient.

Resourcing mathematics learning

In order to implement this way of teaching it is necessary to be well resourced. In particular, each child should have access to materials and activities which model the mathematics to be learnt. Many of these materials already exist in schools and are available from the various distributors of mathematics equipment. Sometimes teachers have needed to make their own resources to fit a specific task being set. To supplement the existing commercial supplies and, in the case of shape, to establish a more comprehensive set of examples, five books—**Triangles**; **Polygons**; **Fractions**; **Numbers and Numerals**; and **Dots and Grids**—provide pages which can be photocopied onto cardboard or paper, cut out and used to resource students' mathematics learning. They will save teachers the time and effort of making these resources for themselves.